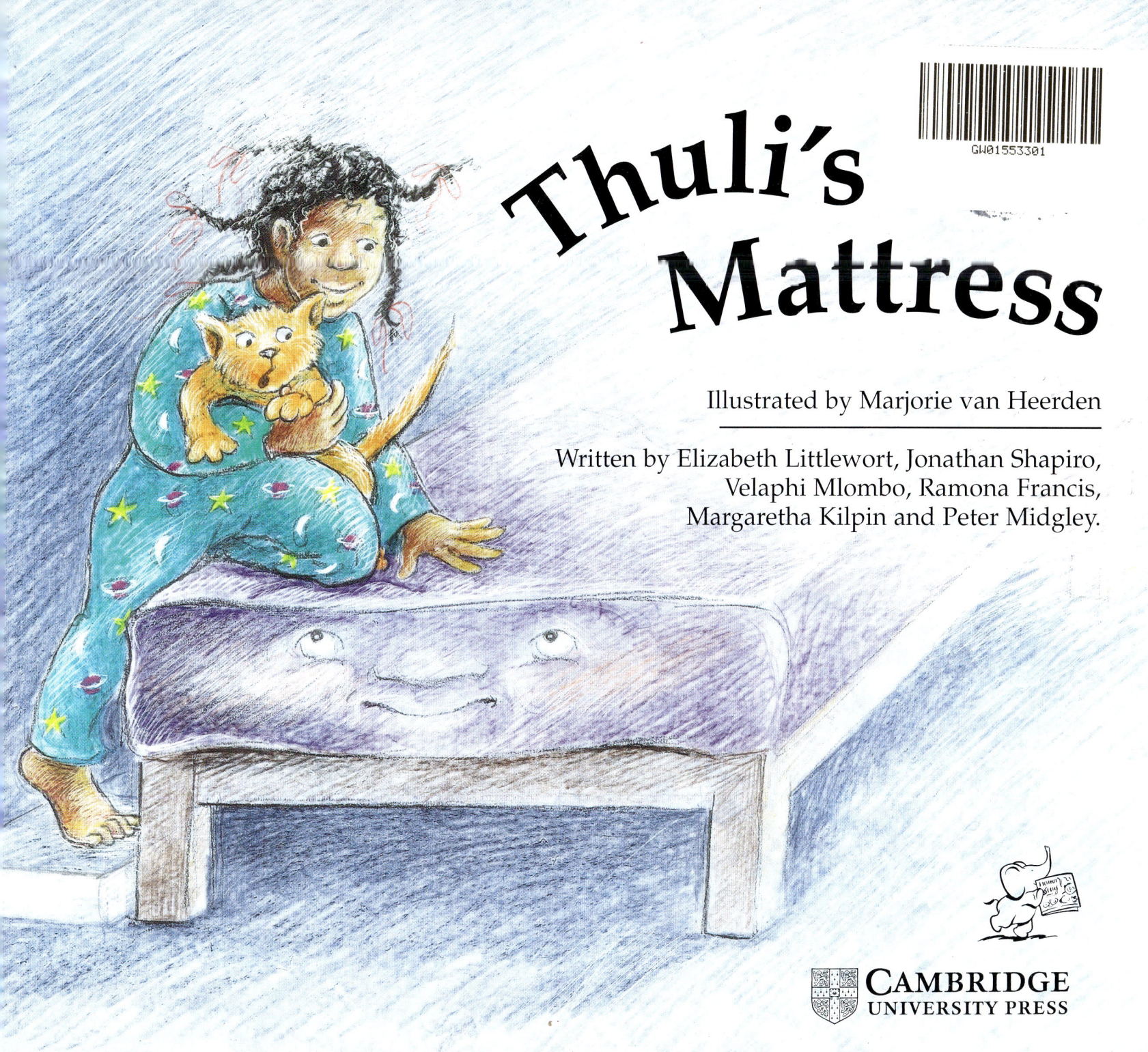

Thuli's Mattress

Illustrated by Marjorie van Heerden

Written by Elizabeth Littlewort, Jonathan Shapiro, Velaphi Mlombo, Ramona Francis, Margaretha Kilpin and Peter Midgley.

CAMBRIDGE UNIVERSITY PRESS

Thuli's mom bought her a new mattress.
"Look at me!" laughed Thuli as she bounced up and down on the mattress.
"Thuli, it's eight o'clock. It's time to go to bed," said her mom.
Thuli lay down and looked out of the window.
Stars twinkled in the sky. One star was specially bright.
"Hmm, I would love to catch that star," thought Thuli sleepily.

Just then, she heard a strange noise.
Her mattress was singing!
"Bounce, bounce, hold on tight!
We will bounce all through the night!"

"Yo! Let's go!" shouted Thuli.

The mattress gave one
    very big bounce ...

and it bounced right out of the window
and over a taxi!
"Wow!" yelled Thuli.

"Bounce, bounce, hold on tight!
We will bounce all through the night!"
sang the mattress.

The mattress landed on top of the house next door!
"Bounce, bounce, hold on tight!
We will bounce all through the night!"

Then the mattress gave a bigger bounce ...

and it bounced on top of a tall building!
"Bounce, bounce, hold on tight!
We will bounce all through the night!"
The mattress gave the
biggest bounce of all.
It rose so high into the sky that Thuli
could see all the buildings in the town beneath her.
The stars sparkled above her.

"Look out! Don't bump into that aeroplane!" yelled Thuli.

As they soared higher and higher,
Thuli could see her star growing
bigger and brighter.
She was close enough to reach out and catch it!
She reached out to grab the star...

but the mattress flopped
down....
down...
down...

The next morning, Thuli woke up.
Her hand was tightly closed.
She opened her hand slowly,
and what do you think she saw?

Then she heard a little voice singing:
"Bounce, bounce, hold on tight!
We will bounce some more tonight!"